MUSIC FEATURED IN THE MOTION PICTURE
THE PIANIST
FOR PIANO SOLO

CONTENTS

Works by Frédéric Chopin

ISBN 978-0-634-06300-8

HAL•LEONARD®
CORPORATION
7777 W. BLUEMOUND RD. P.O. BOX 13819 MILWAUKEE, WI 53213

Visit Hal Leonard Online at
www.halleonard.com

Andante spianato

Frédéric Chopin
1810–1849
Op. 22

This piece is the introduction to Chopin's Grand Polonaise for Piano and Orchestra.

Semplice.

A Monsieur Robert Schumann

Ballade No. 2 in F Major

Frédéric Chopin
1810–1849
Op. 38

Presto con fuoco

A Monsieur le Baron de Stockhausen

Ballade No. 1 in G Minor

Frédéric Chopin
1810–1849
Op. 23

sempre più mosso

Mazurka in A Minor

Frédéric Chopin
1810–1849
Op. 17, No. 4

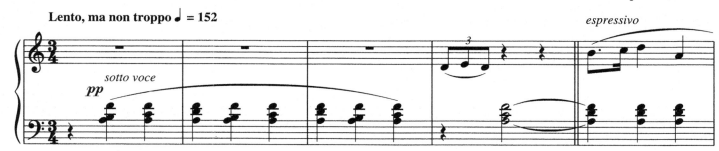

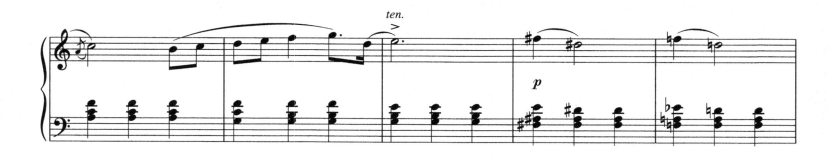

Copyright © 2000 by HAL LEONARD CORPORATION
International Copyright Secured   All Rights Reserved

sotto voce

sempre più piano

calando

perdendosi

Nocturne in C-sharp Minor

Frédéric Chopin
1810–1849
(1830)

Lento con gran espressione

Copyright © 2000 by HAL LEONARD CORPORATION
International Copyright Secured   All Rights Reserved

A Mademoiselle Laura Duperré

Nocturne in C Minor

Frédéric Chopin
1810–1849
Op. 48, No. 1

Nocturne in E Minor

Frédéric Chopin
1810-1849
Op. 72, No. 1

Copyright © 1998 by HAL LEONARD CORPORATION
International Copyright Secured   All Rights Reserved

Prélude in E Minor

Frédéric Chopin
1810–1849
Op. 28, No. 4

A Madame la Baronne C. d'Ivry

Waltz No. 3 in A Minor

Frédéric Chopin
1810–1849
Op. 34, No. 2